LIVING ON THE CHEAP GUIDE

The Ultimate Guide to Coupons

How to Save More Money in Less Time and Get the Best Deals

By Laura Daily and Teresa Mears
(with Bryan K. Chavez)

Published by Mears Media,
4633 Northwest 46th Street,
Tamarac, Florida 33319

ISBN Number: 978-0-9976911-1-5

Written by LAURA DAILY and TERESA MEARS

Cover Illustration by Candace West Photography
http://www.candacewest.com/

Cover Design, Book Design and Production by
Hiram Henriquez, H2H Graphics & Design
http://h2hgraphics.com/

LIVING ON THE CHEAP

www.livingonthecheap.com

Dedication
We dedicate this book to everyone who struggles to make ends meet,
in hope we can make that struggle a little easier.

Acknowledgements
Thanks to everyone who contributed to this book, including
Bryan K. Chavez, Joyce Daily, Shanah Bell, Linda DuVal,
Monica Louie, Jody Mace and Carolyn Erickson.

TABLE OF CONTENTS

OUR STORY

Back in 2008, a freelance writer friend had an idea for a website that would share discounts, deals and free things to do in her local community. Life was expensive, but she knew there were ways to have a good time on less money. She launched our first site, Atlanta on the Cheap.

Readers loved the site, and Atlanta on the Cheap was immediately successful. She came back to our online writers' community and pointed out that what she had done in Atlanta could be done in any city. More than two dozen of her writer friends, including both of us, took up the challenge and our On the Cheap network was born.

We started our sites during the height of the recession, when Americans were struggling to keep their homes and pay their bills, amid rising unemployment and declining assets. But, as we did our research, we discovered that there were lots of free and cheap ways to have fun in every city, plus plenty of ways to get discounts on everything from dining to show tickets.

In 2012, we decided we needed a way to share advice on saving money in one's day-to-day life, how to not just survive but thrive on a budget. So we launched Living on the Cheap, an online personal finance and lifestyle magazine. Keeping with our cheap mantra, our initial site was built by two 50-something journalists talking on the phone between Miami and Denver. You're never too old to learn a new skill. And that includes how to save more money. You're never too young to develop good money habits, either.

Our network now consists of our flagship site, Living on the Cheap, plus more than 25 city sites stretching from Seattle to Miami. The local sites are written and managed by an "in the know" local publisher in each city who shares insider tips on where to go, what to do, where to shop and how to have fun without emptying your wallet. We add new sites every year.

We've read (and written) a lot of articles about saving money using coupons over the years. In putting together this guide, we took into account that your time is valuable, too. Our goal is to provide you with the information you need to save the most money in the least amount of time.

Now that you know us, we hope you'll keep in touch. You can:

• See all of our thrifty living advice at *http://livingonthecheap.com*

• Subscribe to Living on the Cheap's free national newsletter *https://livingonthecheap.com/subscribe*

• Find a local On the Cheap site *https://livingonthecheap.com/our-network/*

• Share your coupon questions at *coupons@livingonthecheap.com*

— Teresa and Laura

LIVING ON THE CHEAP CITY SITES

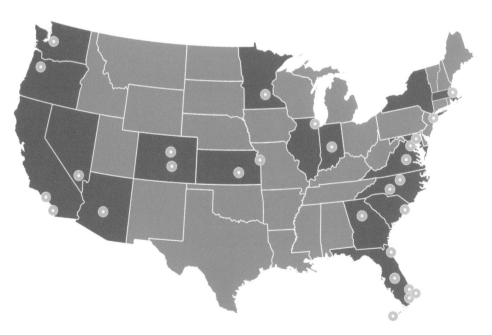

CHAPTER 1
WHY USE COUPONS

Shoppers save more than $3.5 billion annually using coupons on everything from oranges to shampoo to restaurant meals. With just a little time and organization, you can save hundreds or thousands of dollars.

Food, clothing, pet care, going to the movies, even a haircut — everything costs more than it did 10 years ago. But as prices increase, so, too, does our arsenal of tricks to reduce them. Leading the charge is the mighty little coupon.

Some 307 billion coupons were distributed in the United States last year — and that doesn't include digital store coupons loaded directly to your loyalty card. Nearly 90 percent of shoppers say they use coupons — that's about 2.2 billion redeemed — for an annual savings of $3.5 billion. (If every coupon issued were presented at checkout, it would save shoppers $510 billion!)

But it's not just groceries that we can save on. Meals, entertainment, apparel, you name it, and it's likely there is a coupon for it.

True couponers know the secret to savings: equal doses of time (getting organized) and smart shopping. Your greatest deals always come from being a savvy consumer in the grocery aisle. With a few money-saving shopping trips, you could easily have an extra $100 each month in your wallet (or more, if you're really good).

What is it that drives couponers? Sure, everyone likes to save money, or "sale" signs would not be displayed throughout most stores. But for serious savers, the mighty little coupon has become addictive.

So, what makes us crazy for coupons? Is it playing the game — you versus the stores you shop — or the thrill of a "treasure" hunt with the booty bought for pennies on the dollar? Or is it seeing the end of your

receipt say "You saved 95%!" Perhaps you strive to keep every penny in your pocket for future goals, such as vacations or your kids' college educations.

Whatever your motivation, coupons have become a part of our daily lives. Nine out of 10 shoppers use coupons. And — fun fact — more than two-thirds of shoppers buy a product only if there is a coupon for it.

Navigating the coupon world can be tricky. That's why we created this guide. We've compiled the best of "The Coupon Insider" columns from Living on the Cheap with the latest strategies for finding more coupons and using them for maximum savings. Plus, we've added ways to use technology to deliver even more savings.

Even better? There is no need to go to extremes. Forget what you see on those TV shows. (Most of it is rigged anyway with stores overriding cash registers and policies.) You don't have to spend hours every day or fill your basement with 100 boxes of cereal or enough toilet paper to survive a disaster.

Anyone can clip a few coupons out of newspaper inserts, stuff them into an envelope and "maybe" remember to use them at checkout. We're going to take you beyond the basics. A true couponer can buy $100 worth of groceries for $10 or less.

Let's dig in.

How much can you save?

Take a look…

HOW MUCH CAN YOU SAVE?

Yes, these are actual receipts. Check out the one on the left that shows 100%. How about the 101% on the right? We even had a shopping trip when the self-checkout register gave us money at the end of the purchase.

CHAPTER 2
GETTING STARTED

Saving big chunks of money with coupons doesn't require investing big chunks of time. We start with three golden rules that every super-saver must follow to bag the best deals.

Super savers are often asked, "How did you do that?" The secret is that savers are flexible, organized and value money over time. The excuse "I just don't have time" prevents the everyday shopper from being truly committed to saving money at the grocery store. However, once you see how a few hours a week can keep more money in your bank account, it's hard not to get hooked. Are you ready to embrace your inner super saver?

Here are the three golden rules all cheapskates follow when it comes to saving big bucks in the grocery aisle:

GOLDEN RULE #1: YOU CAN'T BE BRAND LOYAL

This tip is probably the most important in saving money at the grocery store. While we all have our favorite foods, flavors and scents, cheapskates believe that most products are the same, regardless of brand. For example, all national brands of shampoo do the same thing — clean your hair. The same holds true for toothpaste, household cleaners, laundry detergent, deodorant and so on.

When you're flexible, you have more options to save money rather than paying full price because "your brand" is not on sale or does not offer a coupon. Remember, companies spend millions on trying to convince you that their product is the best, but think for yourself and be smarter about your grocery dollars.

GOLDEN RULE #2: YOU CAN'T BE LOYAL TO ONE STORE

Much like the don't-be-brand-loyal rule, when you're flexible with where you shop, you widen your money-saving options. We all have our favorites. With stores, it may be because of convenience, customer service or because it's where your family has always shopped.

However, savers know that store sales and promos differ greatly every week. One store may have cereal on sale, while another has bath tissue on sale. Yet another will have discounted dish soap. If you shop at only one store, you're missing out on major savings. (Plus, some stores double coupons, while others do not.)

Take the time to review the weekly circulars before planning a shopping trip. It's easy to get stuck in a shopping habit, but a willingness to break your pattern can keep more money in your pocket. The obvious argument against visiting multiple stores is the cost of gas and time. However, with proper planning, that becomes a non-issue.

In most major cities, competing stores are often within just a mile or two of each other. In some cases, they're right across the street. This is not by coincidence, as many retailers build locations specifically in a competitor's market because they are all fiercely fighting for your business. They need to make it convenient for consumers, so take the time to see what stores you're passing on the way to your favorite.

Many cheapskates map out their shopping plans so they're completing errands efficiently — not running back and forth wasting gas and time. Committed penny-pinchers have been known to make five to six stops in an hour to get their shopping needs met. They are able to do so because they're focused and organized.

GOLDEN RULE #3: WHEN YOU FIND AN AMAZING PRICE, STOCK UP

This requires some patience and storage space, but it's well worth it. When you're a true-blue saver, you're bound to come across some amazing deals. It's not uncommon to get products for free or upward of 75% off. This is the time to stock up on those products your family uses often and that have a long shelf life.

Once, we got Smucker's natural peanut butter for only 25 cents a jar (with a sale and coupon), so why buy just one? We bought 12 and had enough peanut butter for a year — even after sharing a few jars with friends. Some people get nervous about spending more than budgeted on a shopping trip. However, a little extra money spent now on a great price means savings down the road, when you won't have to pay full price for peanut butter.

Unfortunately, this advice doesn't work for perishable foods, unless you're willing to eat the

same thing every meal for a few weeks. The stock-up rule really applies to household cleaners, canned goods, personal hygiene goods, paper products and any household "stuff" you need on a regular basis (trash bags, air fresheners, pet food, etc.) The trick is to check expiration dates, so you're not wasting money on items that will expire before you use them.

Finally, you need to have the space to store your frugal finds. If your storage space is limited, be creative. We've been known to stash canned goods under the bed or in the linen closet. When it's time to restock the kitchen pantry, just go around the house on your very own private "shopping trip."

MAKE IT EDUCATIONAL

Couponing requires math skills. Have the kids sharpen theirs — and learn the value of a dollar — by helping you compute what you'll spend on a shopping trip based on products' prices and the coupons you've got. No calculators allowed!

CHAPTER 3

WHERE TO FIND COUPONS

Coupons are all around. Start with your local newspaper, but don't stop there. You can find coupon inserts in recycling bins, in the mail and even at your favorite coffee shop. And you can even buy discount newspapers.

Where do you find coupons? The most obvious place is the Sunday newspaper (and sometimes Wednesday or Thursday when newspapers include a Food section).

For the best savings, you should have several copies of the same coupon. (Why buy just one box of pasta for 25 cents, when you can get three or four? That's only possible with multiple coupons.)

You could just go out and purchase three or four copies of Sunday's paper, but that will run you up to $10 in most major cities. And, in our "cheap" world, that defeats the purpose of using coupons: to save money. There are a few tricks to getting more coupons at no cost.

DON'T BE SHY

Turn to friends and family for their extras. Even though we wish everyone clipped coupons, most people do not. Every week, most are simply tossed in the garbage or recycle bin. This is like taking money out of your wallet and throwing it away. Ask neighbors or co-workers to save their coupons for you. Then, either make the rounds or arrange a spot for neighbors to leave them on your porch.

SEARCH YOUR COMMUNITY RECYCLE BINS

For many savers, it's a gold mine — just know your city's ordinances before jumping in.

MAKE FRIENDS WITH YOUR NEWSPAPER CARRIER

We know couponers who regularly receive a few extra copies in their Sunday paper, thanks to a generous holiday gift. A $20 bill during the holidays can pay off long-term. Don't offend your delivery person with a "bribe," but it's worth asking just exactly what happens to all of those extra coupons, right?

DOWNLOAD COUPONS

Living On The Cheap has its own coupons page (*http://www.livingonthecheap.com/coupons*) which is updated every few days, and completely restocked at the start of each month. Select the coupons you want and the system will text you a unique code to complete the printing. That security feature is to keep scammers from downloading dozens of the same coupons. You don't need a color printer, but do cut your coupons out neatly so they don't appear to be something you created on a copy machine.

BEFRIEND YOUR FAVORITE BRANDS

In exchange for your email address, companies such as Kellogg's, Johnson & Johnson, Colgate, General Mills and others will email newsletters with recipes or tips and printable high-value online coupons such as buy-one-get-one free.

KEEP YOUR EYES OPEN IN THE STORE

Many coupons can be found right in the grocery aisle. These include Blinkies, a coupon dispenser attached to store shelves (usually with a blinking light to get your attention, hence the name); Peelies, coupons stuck to the product itself that you peel off for instant savings; and Catalinas, coupons that print at checkout (from a Catalina-branded machine) based on your purchases.

LOOK FOR FLIERS

Many fast-food chains include coupon-filled inserts in newspapers or mailings to your home. You'll find similar inserts from retailers such as Family Dollar, Kohl's, Macy's, Ulta and Lowe's.

OPEN YOUR MAIL

Those Valpak coupons you get in the mail are

cart. Next time you're at the grocery store, keep your eyes open and read every sign, flier and tag for hidden savings. You might be surprised at what you find.

BUY DISCOUNT NEWSPAPERS

Even though we love our newspaper, subscription prices have skyrocketed. Don't be lured into buying multiple subscriptions. There are many weekends when newspapers have limited or no coupon inserts. Instead, if you find a week when coupons runneth over, check out your local dollar store. Many sell the Sunday newspaper for just $1, which almost always beats the retail price charged elsewhere.

> ## COUPON INSIDER TIP
>
> The best-kept secret is probably right down the street from you. If you go snooping around on a late Sunday morning (or early afternoon) at your local coffee shop or fast-food restaurant, you can often find a treasure trove of coupons among the Sunday papers left behind by customers. We all see the papers strewn about the tables, sofas and chairs, but few are bold enough to pick them up and rifle through for coupons. Yes, you might get a few weird stares, but who cares? You're saving money! Some of our favorite spots: Starbucks, McDonald's and Panera Bread.

not always the best deals, but you can often find a gem or two. Did you know you can print more coupons at home? Visit the Valpak website (*http://valpak.com*) and enter your location to find printable coupons for merchants in your area — mostly restaurants. However, they have lots of coupons for services, from auto repair to dental care. Each coupon will show the exact location where it's valid, so you know whether or not it's worth printing. You can sort the list by distance or alphabetically. The coupons are updated periodically, so keep checking back for new discounts.

LOOK FOR REBATES

There are many instant rebates when you purchase qualifying products. Many of these promotions are only advertised in the store, often right on the price tag. These offers can be tricky, so always read the fine print before loading up your

CHAPTER 4

MAXIMIZE YOUR SAVINGS

*Use a coupon to get a few cents off a full-price item? You can do better.
Smart coupon use can double or triple your savings.
Sometimes you can even get products free, or close to it.*

It's great to get money off your regular-priced purchase with a coupon, but coupon insiders know even more ways to cut those prices. One easy (and effective) technique is to use coupons for sale-priced items. But there are other secrets to saving, too.

STACK COUPONS FOR MORE SAVINGS

When it comes to coupons, we're always stoked about stacking. What's stacking, you ask? It's when you stack a manufacturer's coupon on top of a store coupon for a double-dip discount.

Many retailers offer store coupons, including most grocery stores, Walgreens, Rite Aid and CVS — just check the weekly ad or inquire at customer service. However, the savings don't stop there because you can also use a manufacturer's coupon on the same item.

True coupon clippers are well-versed in the benefits of stacking, but also know that, for maximum savings, you should stack coupons on top of a sale price when possible. With the combo of stacking and sale prices, you can often get items for free or pennies on the dollar.

Another way to stack is by enrolling in Target Cartwheel. Target lets you add certain offers, typically a percentage discount on various products, and you print them out or keep them on your smart phone. At checkout show the checker the bar code. Then combine with manufacturer's coupons for extra savings. You can also text Target to get mobile coupons.

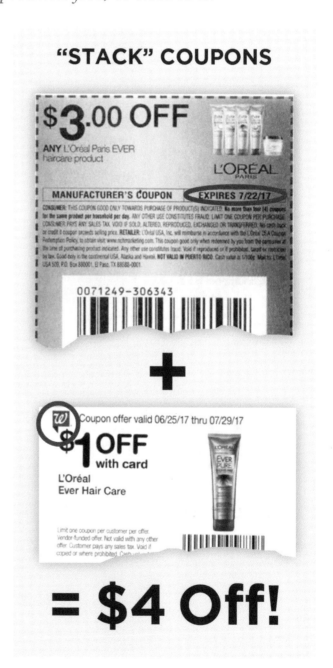

"STACK" COUPONS

$3.00 OFF
ANY L'Oréal Paris EVER haircare product

L'ORÉAL
PARIS

MANUFACTURER'S COUPON   EXPIRES 7/22/17

0071249-306343

+

$1 OFF with card
Coupon offer valid 06/25/17 thru 07/29/17

L'Oréal Ever Hair Care

EVER PURE

Limit one coupon per customer per offer. Vendor-funded offer. Not valid with any other offer. Customer pays any sales tax. Void if copied or where prohibited.

= $4 Off!

DOUBLE THE SAVINGS

Stores that **double** typically do so up to a maximum of $1.

50¢ coupon + 50¢ = **$1 off**
75¢ coupon + 25¢ = **$1 off**
30¢ coupon + 30¢ = **60¢ off**

THE MAGIC OF DOUBLE COUPONS

Couponers know there are more savings to be found in coupons than just face value. What's the trick? Many grocers offer double coupons every day. So, just like magic, a 50-cents-off coupon — poof — turns into $1 off.

Most participating retailers limit the doubling of manufacturer's coupons to a maximum savings of $1, which means coupons up to and including 50 cents off are eligible. Coupons below 50 cents are doubled at face value. (For example, 30 cents off becomes 60 cents off.)

Coupons above 50 cents (and up to 99 cents) are not doubled, but rather extended to reach the $1 maximum limit. (For example, a 55-cents-off coupon will be given an additional 45 cents off for a final savings of $1.) If you're unsure whether your grocer doubles or triples, inquire at the customer service counter.

As with any savings strategy, double coupons can be a bit tricky. It's all in the fine print. Not all coupons are eligible for the promotion. For the most part, digital, store-branded and in-store coupons are not eligible. (By "in-store," we mean coupons you find on shelves or packages.) Our best advice is to just read the coupon — many will clearly state, "Not Subject to Doubling."

BUY LESS, SAVE MORE

Many think bigger is better, but that's not necessarily true. When you use a coupon, the smartest move financially may be to buy the smallest size possible. The savings are in the numbers: Using a $1 off coupon on a $2 box of crackers is a greater discount at 50% off than using the same coupon on a $4 box of crackers for a savings of just 25%.

Still, how do so many couponers get items free? It's all in the fine print. Many coupons state "off any product," which often means there's no size restriction. (Although, to avoid any confusion or frustration at checkout, it's important to double-check coupons for any size or flavor limitations.) In this case, go for the smallest size allowable (often with the smallest price, too) and you could end up with a free item at checkout.

Of course, the best savings always come from combining a sale price with a coupon, which can also lead to a shopping basket full of free or greatly reduced items. For example, once every month or two, grocery stores put a handful of basic items on sale for 99 cents.

These usually include toiletries such as toothpaste, shaving cream, liquid hand soap and toothbrushes. Find coupons that are a match, especially if your retailer doubles coupon values, and you could walk away paying only sales tax on a basket full of goodies.

Next time you're at the grocery store, become a shopping sleuth with notepad in hand: Review tags for sale prices, snoop every shelf for different sizes and pull out a calculator to ensure maximum savings.

SAVE IN THE CLEARANCE AISLE

You can always spot a true cheapskate: We make a beeline for the clearance aisle. For novices, this can be tricky, as the clearance section is not always easy to find. In most cases, it's "hidden" in the store, most often in the back. However, each store is different: Some grocery stores keep clearance items in a corner near the front; others refer to clearance items as "Manager's Specials."

If you can't find the clearance section, ask at the customer service counter — every store has one. You'll know when you find it because it's usually a hodge-podge of products strewn about the shelves. At first, it can be intimidating. However, you can often find some amazing deals. Don't let the clutter deter you from searching for deals.

Items are usually marked at least 50% off — the benchmark for a true frugal find. Now, we know what you're thinking: "It's all expired, old or junk." Not true. Many items make their way to the bargain bin because of overstocking, label changes, seasonal flavors or because they're discontinued.

With a little patience and digging, you can find just about everything from pet food to soup to deodorant and much more. The trick is to check every time you shop, because inventory changes often.

We've been known to take a lazy Saturday afternoon and make a "clearance run" — just shopping the clearance aisles at Target, Walgreens, Rite Aid, Walmart and grocery stores. At the major

stores, what's marked down at one branch is usually marked down at all locations. As a result, we may search just Target stores on a quest for a particular clearance item before it's all gone. It doesn't work each and every time, but it pays off (literally) when you find an unbelievable deal.

Using coupons while shopping the clearance section is one of the main ways cheapskates get items for free or for just a few cents. We have a closet full of soap, toothpaste, shaving cream, shampoo, cereal, soup and more for which we paid pennies.

How do you get started? First, find the clearance aisles in each of the stores you frequent. Then, without fail, check the shelves every time you shop. You might even consider adding "clearance" to your weekly shopping list, as a reminder. Once you make it a habit, it will be second nature for your cart to make its routine pit stop. You'll be amazed at what you find — namely, the money back in your wallet.

COUPON INSIDER TIP

Here's the real secret about clearance aisles: You can use manufacturer's coupons on top of the discounted prices. Some people think coupons can only be used on full-price items. Not true. Marked-down items are fair game for coupon clippers.

You may encounter an employee who questions the policy, but just ask for a manager who should approve the transaction. Why? Because, stores receive the face value of each coupon from the manufacturer, as well as up to an 8-cent handling fee. Be assertive.

CHAPTER 5

REAL MEN USE COUPONS

The True Story of Bryan K.

I had bills to pay, lots of them. I needed to save money. What if my friends found out I was secretly using coupons? Would they think I was too cheap? But once I got started saving, I couldn't stop.

As a human with an XY chromosome, I know there's definitely a stigma to men using coupons. I remember when I first started using coupons after college. I desperately needed to start paying off those credit cards I foolishly maxed out — mostly on bar tabs, concerts and much-too-expensive clothing.

Yes, I, too, succumbed to all those enticements of a free T-shirt or hat in the student center. Little did I know that a free T-shirt could cost thousands of dollars. If I only knew then what I know now. (For the record, I have not carried a credit card balance since graduation.)

Back in those early coupon days, I could feel my mouth drying up, my palms sweating, as I frantically searched for the checkout lane with the fewest customers. If I was lucky, there would be no one. My other requirement was that the clerk had to be a woman. There was no way I was appearing "weak" in front of another guy by using coupons.

Making unnecessary small talk, I nervously handed over my three coupons to the clerk, expecting some sort of unwelcome glance or comment. She simply scanned them with no fanfare and gave me my total. "Well, that was easy," I thought, relieved it was over. I just saved $3. Three whole dollars that I would not have saved otherwise. I was immediately hooked, but the road to out and proud "coupon clipper" was not an easy one.

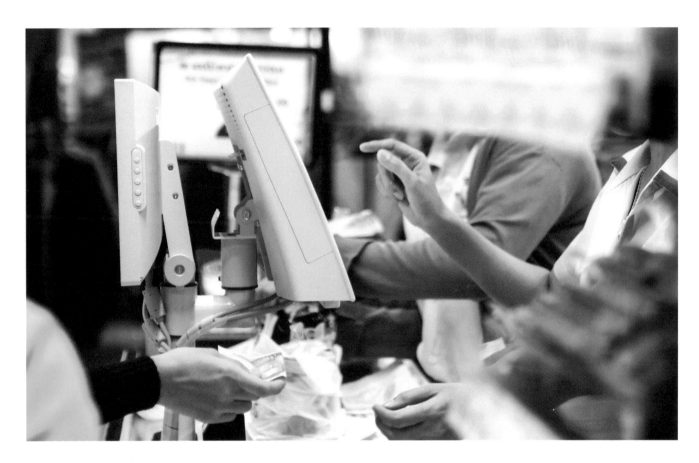

For months, I stood strong on my requirements: an empty checkout lane with a female clerk, which meant many late-night shopping trips. My advantage was that, over time, I was secretly honing my money-saving skills. Coupon clipping is not a subject most sons discuss with their mothers, let alone their fathers. Fathers may talk about the birds and the bees with their male offspring, but they rarely discuss the importance of bargain hunting and budgeting.

In this culture, coupons are often associated with being "cheap" — and "cheap" for men often implies you're not good enough. If a man uses a coupon, he must not be able to afford the full price and, therefore, must not be successful. A daughter, on the other hand, is often groomed from a young age to be a "domestic goddess." A woman uses a

coupon and she's considered a smart shopper. Not true for a man — he uses a coupon and is considered "cheap."

Friends and family started getting suspicious when I would show up with several bags of groceries for less than $10. My biggest allies were the many female clerks I had come to know on a first-name basis. (You know you're getting good when clerks start asking you for advice.)

However, the true revelation, and my acceptance that I was undeniably a coupon clipper, occurred when I paid off more than $4,000 in credit card debt in a little more than a year — an arduous task for someone in his early 20s (actually, at any age.) This feat would not have been possible without coupons.

My secret was starting to get out. Where was I

disappearing to late at night? Where was I getting all this extra money? People started asking questions. I finally gathered enough courage to tell my best friend first, "Yes, I'm a coupon clipper!" And, once he accepted me, I admitted who I truly was to my parents, co-workers and roommates. What a relief to no longer have to keep my coupons tucked away in a shoebox under my bed.

Years later, I proudly carry my coupon file in the store and don't care who's looking. I don't even care about the chromosomes of the clerk. In fact, I'm even so bold as to stop people in the grocery aisle and tell them they could be getting a better price on something in their carts. Many listen, though others turn a deaf ear. I don't care. I'm only trying to spread the gospel of saving money.

Other than reaching my goal of saving 90% on a grocery receipt, my proudest moments as an out-of-the-closet coupon clipper come from the occasional stranger who will stop me in the parking lot and ask for help. (It's important to note that it's always a woman, never a man.)

I love to tell men that there's no shame in using coupons. If being a man means being a good provider, clipping coupons is one of the best ways to do so. How is saving money not being a good provider? For fathers, it's a great opportunity to teach their children about the importance of saving money, building a nest egg and being prepared for life's unexpected turns. (And, for single guys, most partners are looking for a man good with money, right?)

We all want (and need) to save money. Coupons are one of the easiest and quickest ways to reach your financial goals. With coupons, $10 can become $20, $30 or $40 at the grocery store. The trick is to start visualizing coupons as "cash." Once you see the savings, and realize you suddenly have extra money for down payments, college tuition

or a vacation, you'll never look back. There is only power in coupons, not weakness.

Over the years, coupons have changed in many ways, but my passion for them has never waned. I use coupons on just about every purchase I make today, including dining out and going to the movies. I'm not sure the "femininity" of clipping coupons will ever go away, but saving money is so rewarding — whether you're wearing a dress or a suit and tie.

To this day, I have male friends who will still not use coupons because it's embarrassing — even after my numerous lectures. Even in their late 30s, some are always in debt, living in apartments or even back home with their parents. Yet, they still wonder how I made a down payment of 30% on my condo at the age of 30 and have zero credit card debt to this day. Now, where are my scissors?

Trust me, there is no shame or embarrassment in saving money. It's actually one of the smartest moves you can make for you and your family.

— **Bryan K. Chavez**

CHAPTER 6

ORGANIZING YOUR COUPONS

You don't have to devote hours and hours every week to save money with coupons. What you need is a system and a way to make sure you always have the right coupons with you at the right time.

As with any project, the more organized you are, the more successful you'll be. Such is especially true in the world of couponing, particularly if you expect to see any significant savings.

Coupon clippers have their own systems and strategies, but we all have one important trait in common: being organized. This skill is essential in navigating the aisles, literally and figuratively. Without a good system, the process can be overwhelming, laborious and time-consuming.

CUT ONLY COUPONS FOR PRODUCTS YOU USE (OR MIGHT USE)

Beginners often clip every coupon for products from diapers to dog food, but, if you don't have a baby or a dog, it's wasted energy. Just ask yourself before you snip, "Do I use (or need) this product?" Remember you're more likely to save the most money, if you're not brand-loyal.

KEEP ALL LIKE COUPONS IN THE SAME STACK

Once you have your coupons properly stacked, categorize them. This is where you can do what works best for you. The most common form of categorization is by product category, such as frozen food, dairy, canned goods, cereal, personal hygiene, paper products, household cleaners, etc.

However, we've seen systems organized alphabetically by brand. Others have gone so far as to order their coupons based on the aisle layout of their favorite grocery store. Just find an organizational system that works for you and stick with it.

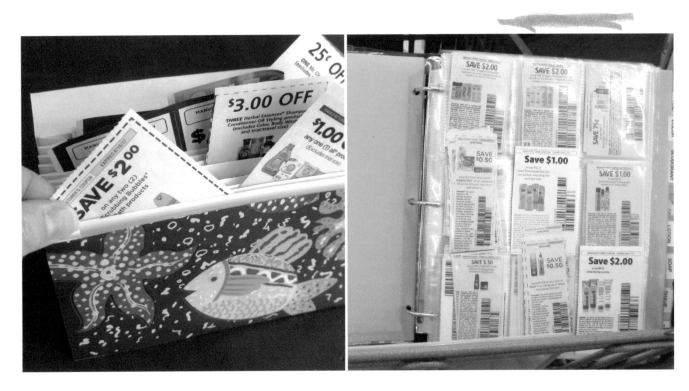

KEEP ALL COUPONS IN ONE SPOT

Use a coupon file, a binder with pockets or even a small bin. You simply need to find a storage system that is easy to maintain, as well as transport to and from the store. To avoid losing your coupon file — a heartbreaking experience for any true cheapskate — choose a bright (even neon) color, so you're not likely to leave it in the shopping cart or misplace it. Plus, it never hurts to place an "If found, please contact" sticker prominently on the front.

ONCE YOU HAVE A SYSTEM, NEVER LEAVE HOME WITHOUT IT

The most common excuse we hear from family and friends as to why they don't use coupons is "I always forget them." This is a good reason to keep your file in the back seat or trunk of your car. You never know when you'll find a great sale price and can save even more with a coupon — only to realize you've left them at home. Bring it in the house once a week for maintenance (adding new coupons and trashing expired ones), but then put it right back in the car.

COUPON INSIDER TIP

If you always want to have your coupons at hand, use the binder method. Buy a three-ring binder and plastic sheets used to hold collectible baseball cards. They are the perfect size to hold coupons. Sort your coupons by category. The binder balances perfectly on your shopping cart and you never have to worry about forgetting that you have a coupon for a specific product as you simply flip through to the corresponding category as you shop store aisles. Also, this method makes it easy to toss expired coupons.

CHAPTER 7

DIGITAL OR PAPER?

Yes, you can get coupons on your phone, and you should. But paper coupons sometimes can get you more savings – even if you print them out from your computer. Who says you can't use both and save more?

With nearly everyone owning a smartphone, digital coupons have become increasingly popular. It makes sense. With the flick of a finger, you can search for and add manufacturer's coupons to your shopper's card — anytime, anywhere.

While they offer convenience and are environmentally friendly, digital coupons are typically exempt from double-coupon promotions. In other words, you can't double that 50-cent digital coupon to $1. And, you can usually use only one, though these days some stores allow for multiple uses (typically up to four times).

For most committed couponers, paper coupons are still the way to go. Not only can they be doubled up to $1 at stores offering such savings, you can use more than one at checkout. At certain stores, you can use several of the same coupon on as many qualifying products.

COUPON INSIDER TIP

To avoid any confusion or embarrassment, get a copy of your store's coupon policy before shopping. It's usually available at the customer service desk or online. Each store has different rules beyond the actual coupon.

Plus, you can stack store coupons on top of manufacturer's paper coupons. In the end, the savings can be more bountiful with paper coupons.

Paper coupons may take more effort than digital, but they pay off at checkout with increased savings. Remember, you can't stack paper coupons on top of digital coupons, if they're both manufacturer's coupons. On the flip side, you can stack store coupons on top of manufacturer's digital coupons.

CHAPTER 8

GET TO KNOW YOUR COUPONS

Reading the fine print can often reveal deals you didn't realize were available from just looking at the photos. It's important to know how each coupon can be used to maximize your savings. And, don't be fooled by fakes.

To maximize your coupons, you MUST get used to reading the fine print. Here's one example.

This toothbrush coupon (at right) lists three basic models that you can't use the coupon on, but not Colgate Triple Action. When those toothbrushes go on sale for $1, you can bet we are using this coupon to save big.

Be sure to double-check limits. One coupon per purchase means you can only use one coupon per item. In this case, note that the coupon below also limits you to two identical items in the same shopping trip. Most coupons have a four-item limit, but Unilever (maker of Suave, AXE, Dove, Tresemme, etc.) typically limits you to two on its products, as does Procter & Gamble (maker of Crest, Tide, Pantene, Bounty, etc.).

Double-check limits

Does NOT "exclude" Triple Action

And this may sound nuts, but consider carrying a magnifying glass. Why? Here's one coupon (below) that caused a ton of confusion for shoppers and checkers alike. It says $1 off Gillette Satin Care or Venus Shave Gel, both for women. But there is a picture of men's shaving cream as well and we saw shoppers using the coupon for that. Can you spot the hiccup?

Yes, that little comma after the word Gillette, which so many missed. That's the reason why the shelves were brimming with men's shave gel and the product for women was gone.

Just because there's a picture doesn't mean the coupon is just for that product. Of course, manufacturers want you to buy their most expensive brand. The coupon at right pictures the more expensive varieties of toothpaste. But the coupon is good for ANY Colgate toothpaste over 4 ounces. So when Colgate toothpaste drops to 99 cents, you can bet we are stocking up.

Similarly, here is a great deal (next page) on razors, $2 off any BIC disposable.

We found BIC Silky Touch for $2.99, but it isn't pictured on the coupon. Needless, to say the poor checker was completely flummoxed, though in the end, after checking with his manager, he scanned it and, of course, the register accepted it.

AVOID FAKE COUPONS

With the popularity of reality TV shows promoting "extreme couponing," there has been an increase of fraudulent "free product" coupons. You are most likely to find them for items of high value ($5 or more), such as toilet paper, paper towels, bacon, batteries and more.

As a serious coupon clipper, it's important to play by the rules. You can still save lots of money, buy items individually or by the case, use hundreds of coupons and leave the store saving 99% on your receipt, all in a single transaction.

You don't want to get caught at the checkout for committing fraud by unintentionally using a fake coupon. Many stores are cracking down on this behavior by contacting store security and/or the police on the spot. The embarrassment and

repercussions are simply not worth saving a few bucks.

How do you spot a fraudulent coupon? Manufacturers have become smarter about distributing and identifying legitimate ones. Free or high-value coupons usually have holograms, watermarks, heat-sensitive areas, serial numbers and/or some other means for retailers and customers to authenticate the coupon. If yours doesn't have something similar, it could be a fake.

According to the Coupon Information Center, a nonprofit association of consumer-product manufacturers dedicated to fighting coupon fraud, here are some ways to avoid fake coupons:

• Never pay for coupons.

• Beware of e-mails and Facebook posts containing high-value coupons, no matter the source. (Just because Grandma forwarded you an email with a free coupon doesn't mean it's legitimate.)

• Avoid coupons posted to online discussion forums.

• Avoid any photocopied coupons. That's a no-no.

• If you do print coupons at home (a legitimate practice), check your computer screen. The coupon itself should not be visible. Legitimate coupon distribution systems "cloak" the coupons so while you can view a progress bar that says "your coupons are printing," you won't see the coupon itself.

• Concerned that you may have a fake? You can always check this list of current counterfeit coupons (*http://www.couponinformationcenter. com/psa-list.php*).

The Coupon Information Center has even developed Considerate Couponing Guidelines to better explain the legalities, responsibilities and etiquette of coupons for both consumers and retailers.

DOUBLE-CHECK THAT RECEIPT

After spending time organizing your shopping trip for maximum savings, your work is not quite done. The final and most important step is to review your receipt. There's no benefit in shopping smart only to find out you did not receive a sale or promo price. (Grocery stores often say pricing errors are due to computer systems not being updated.) While statistics are difficult to find, it happens to shoppers every day and they have no idea because they're too busy to review their receipts. Maybe it's even happened to you.

We regularly find overcharges — probably once or twice a week. Usually, it's because an expired sales tag has been left on the shelf. (However, most stores will honor the posted sale price. If not, just return the item on the spot.)

Rarely, an item is simply tagged with an old or incorrect regular price — but it happens. Another common mistake is getting charged twice for the same item. Today's scanners are extremely sensitive, so an unfocused clerk can easily scan an item twice without even knowing it — especially on large shopping orders.

The most frustrating errors are the promos or specials, such as "buy this, get this for free" or "buy three of these, get additional savings." These seem to be the offers with which many consumers have the most trouble, namely because employees are unaware of the details.

It's always helpful to have the ad in hand or picture of the promo sign on your phone. It's also important to ensure you receive the proper pricing on clearance and "manager's specials." You'd be surprised at the number of times we've been charged full price.

While customer service is usually good when dealing with pricing errors, it can become frustrating and time-consuming — especially if you don't resolve the problem immediately. If you go back a few days later (or, even worse, a week later), you're likely to have more of a challenge — as sale prices have changed, tags have been removed or promos have ended. All of this makes it more difficult for store personnel to verify the price. The quicker you address the problem, the better the outcome.

Checking your receipt immediately upon checkout is wise because not only is your memory fresh, but, if you find an error, you don't have to spend the time and gas going back for resolution. It can even pay off, as some stores have a "scan guarantee policy." If an item rings up at a higher price than tagged or advertised, they'll give it to you for free.

Try to catch pricing errors right at checkout to save time. Also watch closely to ensure every coupon is being scanned. It can be a struggle with so much noise and chaos at checkout, but it's worth it. In any case, always double-check your receipt before leaving the store.

CHAPTER 9

RACK UP THE SAVINGS WITH APPS

Of course there's an app for that. While paper coupons often yield top savings, new apps are emerging that will help you save even more. Some apps will yield additional savings or rebates on top of your coupon deals.

The everyday purchases are the ones that will get us — necessities we purchase on a regular basis such as food, toilet paper, cleaning supplies and soap. So consider making a conscious effort to cut back costs on these. There are a ton of phone apps that can help increase your savings, and new ones come out every day. It can be hard to weed through them all to find the ones that offer the greatest benefit. Here are some worth investigating.

EBATES

Ebates is one of the largest sites devoted to getting you cash back on items you would already buy, from household products to cosmetics and, yes, even grocery staples. Ebates rewards members with cash back every time they shop online through the Ebates portal. It also features "hot deals" and coupons for popular stores such as Kohl's, Macy's, Shutterfly and more. You can sign up at for Ebates at *https://livingonthecheap.com/ ebates*.

For groceries and household items, you can get cash back from Jet.com and Walgreen's and coupons from Safeway. If you download the Ebates app (compatible with most smart phones), you can use in-store coupons, scan products to compare prices and get regularly updated deals.

IBOTTA

Looking for something a little simpler than Ebates? Check out *Ibotta*, which flat-out rewards you for grocery shopping and more. Ibotta is a free mobile coupon app, compatible with most smart phones, where shoppers are able to earn cash back on certain products by performing simple tasks such as answering a one-question survey or watching a 15-second video, purchasing the product, then providing proof of purchase.

Ibotta is a terrific app to have when grocery shopping because you can use it to get cash back on things you were already planning to buy, including basics such as milk, bread and produce (with these items you can buy any brand). It's also very simple

to use, and you can unlock cash-back rewards even while you're waiting in line at the grocery store. Best of all, Ibotta doesn't care how you pay for items. Its rebates are on top of savings earned through sales and/or using coupons.

Millions of shoppers use Ibotta and the app has recently completed a total overhaul to make it even easier to use. Ibotta is full of rebates at nearly 150 major retailers, for which you earn cash that you can withdraw once you hit $20. You can either have the money deposited into your PayPal account or you can redeem the money for gift cards.

To unlock the rebates, find the store that you plan to shop at to see which rebates it has and hit the plus sign next to any product you may purchase, and the products are automatically added to your list. Buy the item at that store. In the app, take a photo of the receipt. Ibotta makes it easy to take a picture of a long receipt by allowing you to do it in segments. It then automatically merges them into a single image.

In some cases you have to also scan the actual product's barcode, though eventually you won't have

to do that. But the revised app makes that simple as well and automatically captures the barcode without you having to push any buttons — just point and it does the work. Then you submit the receipt and, after your purchase is verified, Ibotta credits your account. This usually takes 24 hours or less.

This app also works with loyalty cards and doesn't require the steps outlined above after purchase if you tie those cards to your Ibotta account. The rebates are deposited into your account within 48 hours.

As a bonus, you can earn $5 for every friend you invite and Ibotta has different teamwork bonuses every month for people on your team.

Living On The Cheap testers who have used Ibotta find that sometimes it is glitchy — you may have to transmit your receipt more than once — but the upgrade has streamlined the rebate process and the number of rebate partners continues to grow. Once you get the hang of Ibotta, you can certainly earn extra cash on top of your coupon savings.

You can sign up for Ibotta at *https://living onthecheap.com/Ibotta*.

COUPON INSIDER TIP

Take the money, deposit it into your PayPal account, and then transfer it to your bank account. Then withdraw the cash and put it in your grocery envelope to increase your grocery fund for the month.

TARGET CARTWHEEL

Cartwheel is a mobile coupon app specifically for Target, and offers special coupons and discounts only for customers using the app. You won't even know about these discounts unless you download the app at *https://cartwheel.target.com*.

Target's Cartwheel app lets you search for deals ahead of time, but you can also scan things in the store as you pick them up to see if there is a deal on those or similar products.

There's no clipping coupons, plus deals are updated weekly and daily. No wi-fi on your phone? No problem, as most Targets now offer free guest wi-fi. With Cartwheel you have no excuses not to save money on (almost) every Target purchase you make.

WALGREENS

Walgreen's is a top-notch drugstore app (*https://livingonthecheap.com/walgreensapp*). Not only is it easy to use but there are some great deals to be had. The home screen layout is easy to navigate, and it's best to start with the "Weekly Ad & Coupons" section. When you find products of interest, simply tap the "Clip to Card" button. This adds it to your rewards card to use the next time you're in the store.

For specific products, use the "Shop Products" portion of the app to see whether the store has the item and at what price. This app also allows you to rack up rewards points that turn into money. When you combine the rewards cash, the clipped coupons in the app and the Ibotta rebates, savings go through the roof!

RECEIPT HOG

Receipt Hog (*https://receipthog.com*) doesn't care where you shop, as it just wants you to take a picture of your receipts and rate your visit. There are different levels of rewards for big-box stores, gas stations, specialty stores, grocery stores, etc.

You can take a picture of any receipt within a two-week period and it will be credited to your account. Once you hit 1,000 coins, you can redeem them for a $5 Amazon gift card or get a deposit to your PayPal account. If you hit 2,900 coins, it turns into $15. A total of 4,300 coins turns into $25, and 6,500 coins turns into $40.

FAVADO

Favado is a simple (*https://www.savings.com/favado*) created by Savings.com. It aggregates coupons from around the web, which includes the paper coupons released in the Wednesday circulars, and puts them all in the app for you to see quickly. Simply click "add" to whichever coupon you want to use on your next grocery trip, and Favado will save that coupon for you.

You may need to print some coupons at home before grocery shopping, so be sure to check before you go out. Best of all, Favado connects with Ibotta to let you know if you can get additional Ibotta points, essentially getting you an even better discount with cash back.

Favado is very easy to set up after downloading. Simply enter your zip code, watch the stores around you pop up, then check all the stores where you frequently shop. Yes, you can check every single store around you to see all the coupons and collect the best deals.

SHOPKICK

Shopkick is a fun app (*https://www.shopkick.com*) that rewards you with points that can be redeemed for gift cards to your favorite stores. Shopkick rewards you for walking into stores, or around stores if you're in a mall, scanning items and purchases.

Shopkick is similar to Ibotta, except you don't have to buy anything at all to get rewarded. Yes, really, all you have to do to get rewarded by Shopkick is walk around a store, which makes it a great way to get extra exercise and get paid for it.

Shopkick also rewards you with "kicks" (points to redeem for gift cards) on tons of grocery items, from yogurt to wine to coffee.

CHAPTER 10

WAYS TO SAVE BEYOND COUPONS

Coupons are one way to save money on food and household products, but they're not the only way to save. Try these additional techniques, and see how much farther your money will go.

Coupons are one way to save money on groceries and household items, but they're not the only way.

What's as effective as using coupons? Strategic shopping, or buying the things you use when they are on sale. Ideally, you'll purchase these staple items in large enough quantities to last until the next sale. If done correctly, smart shopping should save you way more than buying at full price with coupons.

Start by identifying the 10 or 15 items your family uses most often, with emphasis on the more expensive ones, tracking their prices and how often they go on sale. When the items go on sale, buy enough to last until the next sale.

If, for example, chicken breasts go on sale every other week for half the normal price, buy two weeks' worth and freeze the extras.

One way to save on produce is to buy what's in season: watermelon and berries in summer and citrus in winter, for example.

But even nonperishable items have a sale season. Canned soup, baking supplies, cold medicines, canned fruits and vegetables, baking supplies and oatmeal all appear at their lowest prices in winter. Those items may go on sale in summer, but not as often, and the price may not be as good. And, when those items are in season, you're more likely to find coupons that will take the price even lower.

Summer products include condiments,

barbecue sauce, hot dog and hamburger buns, sunscreen, adhesive bandages and antibiotic spray. As Valentine's Day approaches, look for sales on steak and potatoes, which will be discounted because of the number of couples planning to cook a romantic meal at home.

If you really want to ramp up your savings, use these strategic shopping tactics WITH coupons.

Here are 10 ways to save money on groceries beyond clipping coupons.

1 BUY WHAT'S ON SALE

This is the single best tip for most shoppers. Meat, bread, produce, condiments, coffee, cereal, pet food – nearly everything goes on sale from time to time. Many products go on sale at regular intervals. Find out when your favorite

grocery items go on sale, and try to buy just enough until you can get the next discount.

2 BUY WHAT'S IN SEASON

This goes for both produce and nonperishable goods. Don't plan a dish that requires fresh mango in winter, when the fruit is more expensive. Instead, focus on oranges because they're actually in season.

3 USE WHAT YOU BUY

Many families end up throwing away significant quantities of food, either because they get tired of leftovers or they don't use items before they go bad. You can freeze or repurpose leftovers. Use leftover mashed potatoes to make shepherd's pie, for example. You can also freeze most things not used immediately, including many fresh fruits and vegetables. If you're faced with a pile of broccoli and a bag of potatoes, visit your favorite recipe website with a "search by ingredient" section to find recipes for a meal with what you have on hand.

4 DON'T BUY MORE THAN YOU NEED

A great sale is no deal if you end up throwing away half of what you bought. If you find yourself routinely throwing out produce, bread and meat, then you are buying too much. Plus, not all items last forever, even if they're unopened. Cereal and crackers won't last long in humid climates, and family tastes may change as well.

5 USE STORE LOYALTY PROGRAMS

Many stores require you to have a loyalty card to take advantage of sale prices. The cards are free and usually issued on the spot. Some programs give you bonuses, like discounts on gas, for using your card. Many allow you to "clip" coupons online and store them on your card, giving you an automatic discount at checkout.

6 SHOP AT DISCOUNT GROCERY STORES

Aldi and Save-A-Lot are expanding to more cities, and those no-frills stores can provide some good deals on staples, including produce. Some of their store-brand products also are quite good.

7 TRY ALTERNATIVES TO YOUR USUAL STORE

Most people have access to at least two grocery stores, as well as Walmart, Target and perhaps a discount grocery or ethnic market. Visit other stores from time to time to see if they offer your favorite items at a price worth making an occasional special trip.

8 LEARN THE SALE CYCLES OF YOUR FAVORITE PRODUCTS

If you live in an area with multiple supermarkets, the same products will go on sale, but not at the same time. If you missed the half-price Cheerios at Kroger last week, you may find them at Safeway this week. If your family eats a lot of yogurt, pay attention to how often your favorite brand goes on sale at the best price and stock up then.

9 ASK ABOUT MARKDOWNS

Talk to your store's department managers in meat, dairy, seafood and baked goods to find out if there is a time of day that unsold products are marked down.

Find the store clearance rack. Discontinued products are often sold for half-price or less in sale bins. And, if you need to clip, you can use coupons for these items.

10 BUY STORE BRANDS

Store brands of canned vegetables, cat food, paper products and many other items often are the same products sold under brand names. It's unlikely that you'll notice any difference.

CHAPTER 11

STRETCHING GIFT CARDS

Don't think that a $25 gift card is worth only $25. With some smart shopping, you can stretch your gifts cards into covering far more than face value. And maybe you'll want to buy yourself a few "gifts," too.

Gift cards remain one of the most wanted gifts, no matter the occasion. Even though they're plastic, if you play your (gift) cards right, you can really stretch them beyond their value. The trick is to treat them like cash. Would you be so quick to spend a $50 bill sitting in your pocket? Probably not.

Don't treat a gift card any differently than you would the rest of your budget. It's easy to splurge on a high-ticket item with a card received as a gift. However, just because you purchased a $100 shirt for $50 out-of-pocket (thanks to the $50 gift card you received) doesn't mean you saved money. In fact, you still paid full price.

The smart shopper uses her gift card in conjunction with store discounts, coupons or sales. By doing so, you can quickly increase its value — even doubling it. The best example is restaurant gift cards. We never use a restaurant gift card without a coupon, menu special or promo — just as we would if we were paying cash. With the right buy-one-get-one free coupons, you can easily turn a $50 restaurant gift card into $100.

For store gift cards, suppress the urge for immediate gratification and wait for the next big sale or promo. Better yet, shop the clearance aisles and really stretch it. Or if you are shopping online, check Living on the Cheap's Store Promo Codes page (*https://livingonthecheap.com/PromoCodes*) to find codes worth extra discounts from major retailers. Then, pay using your gift card. While you may not be able to double a gift card's value every

time, with a little patience and planning, you can definitely squeeze a few more dollars out of it.

And who says gift cards must be gifts? The holiday season is the best time to invest in yourself and your favorite retailers. Many stores and restaurants offer bonuses and/or discounts for purchasing gift cards starting in mid-November through the end of December. To save money all year long, purchase gift cards during the holidays from the businesses you frequent often. By doing so, you can "cash in" on free meals, bonus gift cards or gifts with purchase.

If you are going to spend money on lunch at Olive Garden anyway, why not get a few free desserts in the process? Most gift cards do not have an expiration date, so you can redeem them months or years later. (It's especially a great idea to buy gift cards for those restaurants that are your go-to spots

for work lunches or family dinners and redeem the bonus offers after the first of the year.) Remember, it's not a deal, if you can't use the freebie — so be sure to review the restrictions on bonus cards first.

As gift-givers and true cheapskates, we like to buy gift cards for others, but, truth be told, we often keep the bonuses for ourselves as an added — well, bonus. However, we never like to see others waste money, so enclose coupons for the retailer or restaurant along with the respective gift card. It's an easy and convenient reminder for my loved ones to spend the gift card wisely.

If you received a gift card from a retailer you don't like, consider selling it on the many websites that buy unwanted gift cards. Be warned, you may only get half the face value. For a bigger cut, you can sell it on eBay. Best of all, don't assume there's nothing you want from the store. Check out

the website or visit a store — you just might find something you like and get the gift card's full value. If not, consider shopping for a gift for someone else and pay using the "unwanted" gift card. In the end, you'll save money by not having to pay cash for a birthday or wedding gift.

COUPON INSIDER TIP

It's estimated $2 billion worth of gift cards go unredeemed annually. So, if you're on the receiving end of a gift card, don't just toss it in a drawer. Keep it in your wallet, so you're more likely to remember to use it.

CHAPTER 12

BEYOND THE GROCERY STORE

Coupons aren't just for groceries and household products. You can find ones for clothing, furniture, restaurants, attractions — you just have to know where to look. Hint: Don't throw away your mail.

IT'S A WORLD OF COUPONS

Coupons aren't limited to the grocery aisle. Bargain hunters know they're everywhere and available for nearly everything under the sun. That's why they never pay full price for anything — groceries, dining out, going to the movies, recreation or gifts. Every business is in aggressive competition for consumer dollars, so coupons have become extremely important in getting customers through the doors. Smart shoppers use that to their advantage.

For beginners, the trick is to think of coupons as cash. If you saw a $5 bill sitting on a shelf, you wouldn't pass it up. There are coupons all around in plain sight, if you simply open your eyes. It's a new world now — many coupons no longer have a dotted line, are printed on paper or distributed in the ways of the past. Just like cheapskates, coupons come in all shapes and sizes.

SIGNED, SEALED & DELIVERED

Everyone gets (and hates) junk mail. However, there can be gold in many of those coupons you throw away. Don't be so quick to toss out those blue envelopes or local coupon books. While many of the coupons offer little value, you can always find a gem or two. Look for BOGOs, grand opening specials or gifts with purchase. A few seconds of sifting through can save big bucks on

entertainment and dining.

Sign up for mailing lists for your favorite store or restaurant. While most offers are now digital, you can still expect to receive the occasional coupon or promo postcard via snail mail. These coupons tend to be of high value, as they're limited in quantity and cannot be easily shared via social media, unlike their digital counterparts.

RECEIPT REQUIRED

It pays to look at your receipt — front AND back. First, always double-check your receipt to ensure you've been charged correctly. Then, flip it over for more savings. Most grocery store receipts have coupons on the back for local businesses, many a few blocks or steps away.

Often, you'll find deals for liquor stores, hair salons, coffee shops and fast-food chains right in the neighborhood or the same shopping center as the grocery store. Don't be shy! If you see a receipt on the ground or hanging out of the trash can, pick it up just as you would a dollar bill.

Also, when you're done dining (whether it's fast-food or five-star), look at the bottom of your receipt. Many restaurants offer deals if you bring the receipt on your next visit or reward you with savings for completing a survey.

EXTRA! EXTRA!

Tons of manufacturers' coupons are included in the Sunday paper. However, if you rifle through all of the inserts, you're bound to find more than grocery deals. (Many newspapers also place inserts with the grocery ads on Wednesdays or Thursdays.) Many fast-food chains insert coupons, usually promoting their latest menu item or meal deal, including Arby's, Burger King, Carl's Jr./Hardee's, McDonalds, Wendy's and more. The inserts almost always have coupons good for BOGOs or half-price food.

It doesn't end with food. Many department stores and big-box retailers include coupon inserts for bonus savings, percentage-off or dollar-off deals. You'll likely find coupons often for Ace Hardware, Kohl's, Jo-Ann Fabrics, Macy's, Michaels, Ulta and more.

Also, review all the store ads and inserts, as many now include store coupons in the circular, including Rite Aid, Target and Walgreens. A few extra minutes nosing through your newspaper can deliver lots of savings.

LOYALTY PAYS

Just about every business and restaurant offers some sort of loyalty club, almost exclusively digital. First, it's best to set-up a "dummy email account" only for e-clubs and newsletters. Otherwise, your inbox will be overwhelmed, and reading your e-mail every morning will be an arduous task.

To get in on the action, sign up for every club or e-newsletter for those places you frequent often. (Even better, consider businesses you don't frequent often, so you're in the know in case of an amazing deal, great freebie or once-a-year coupon offering big savings.)

This strategy pays off deliciously for restaurants. Many eateries send one-time, exclusive coupons to their subscribers every month or week. Plus, expect to get the best coupons when they're promoting a new menu item or seasonal menu – maybe a buy-one-get-one free entrée.

For stores, expect to receive access to members-only sales, advance notice of sales or promos and exclusive coupons.

Save on paper and ink, as most e-club coupons can be redeemed by simply showing the coupon on your smartphone.

RACK 'EM UP

We all pass the racks at the store entrance without a second thought. You're missing out on lots of savings when you do. Many city newspapers, trade magazines or shopping guides have coupons waiting just for you. Flip through the pages and you're sure to find discounts for many local shops and/or locally-produced products.

Many stores offer books full of store coupons right at the front door — many not found in the general circulars. These coupons are typically good for an entire month and switch out at the beginning of each month. (The best example is Walgreens, which offers a monthly savings book full of coupons.

You'll also find them at stores such as Bed, Bath & Beyond.)

It never hurts to ask. If you don't see any coupons, ask an employee. You never know what you might uncover.

BY THE BOOK

One of the best bets for savings is the *Entertainment Book (https://ivingonthecheap.com/Entertainment Book)*. Available for most major U.S. cities, the book is chock full of deals on entertainment and local food. Even better, the company offers deals on the books (as low as $5) on a regular basis, so never pay the full price of $35. The book pays for itself with the use of just a few coupons. Many bargain hunters purchase a few books to have one handy in each car, or for home and work. Frugal travelers have also been known to buy one for their destination city. Just because you're on vacation doesn't mean you have to throw frugality out the window.

The Entertainment Book may be one of the biggest, but it's not the only coupon book in town. Nowadays, there are coupon books available via apps, fundraisers, shopping malls, websites — all offering deals right in your neighborhood. (At the shopping mall, stop by the customer service counter and ask. Many offer coupon books for new shoppers.)

You might even stop by your local tourist office or attractions and search for coupons. There's no rule that says you can't be a "tourist" in your own city.

Finally, if you see someone using a coupon at a local business or restaurant, ask where they found it. Fellow cheapskates can be the best resource.

DAILY DOUBLE

Well-versed frugal shoppers know about the benefits of Groupon *(https://livingonthecheap.com/Groupon)* and Living Social *(https://livingonthecheap.com/*

LivingSocial), but there are more daily deal sites to be found in your own backyard. Many major cities have daily deal sites managed by local newspapers or radio stations.

It's one of the easiest ways to double your money, as most offers are 2-for-1 or 50% off. Snoop around on your local newspaper and radio websites for potential deals as well as at Living on the Cheap *(https://livingonthecheap.com)* and your local On the Cheap site *(https://livingonthecheap.com/our-network)*. A voucher is the same as a coupon — you're just pre-paying for goods or services.

IN THE END

The trick is to get into the mindset of never paying full price. Always ask if there's a coupon or discount available. Die-hard couponers are always prepared and very resourceful. Start a coupon file, so you're never at a loss searching for coupons at the last minute.

Categorize it by business (McDonald's, Target, Walgreens, etc.) or category (fast-food, casual dining, drugstore, etc.) — whatever works best for you. And, the best tip of all, keep a pair of those small folding scissors in your glove box, bag or file — you never know when you're going to need to do some quick clipping.

HALF-PRICE TICKETS

Tickets to professional theater, concerts and sporting events can be pricey, if not downright out of reach for many. That's one reason why Goldstar *(https://livingonthecheap.com/Goldstar)* is so appealing.

The company works with entertainment companies and venues to sell excess tickets to theater, concerts, comedy shows and sports. Often the ticket discounts are as much as 50% off. Buying tickets is easy and straightforward. There are service charges, but they are clearly noted.

CHAPTER 13

USING COUPONS TO DINE OUT FOR LESS

If you like to eat out, you're in luck. Restaurants make plenty of coupons available to get diners in the door. Join email and loyalty clubs and keep your eyes on social media if you want to eat out at a discount.

If you like to dine out, coupons are your new best friends. You can find coupons for discounts, or even free meals, from restaurants ranging from fast-food to fancy. Thanks to technology, it only takes a few minutes to search for dining specials or coupons.

USE SOCIAL MEDIA AND EMAIL

Sign up for a restaurant's loyalty or insider club. You'll be privy to upcoming discounts, coupons and 2-for-1 specials. These days, most restaurants have some sort of email club, even if it's not advertised.

When dining out, look for signs, read the menu or ask a staff member about such programs. Check a restaurant's Facebook page or Twitter account (especially for local, independent spots), as many share deals and discounts via social media with "friends and family." You may also find deals on Yelp.

You'd be surprised at how quickly you'll start receiving goodies in your inbox. Many businesses offer freebies or discounts just for registering. Most offer a freebie on your birthday. Read offers carefully. Many have short expiration dates. Pace yourself. Don't sign up for too many at one time. Otherwise, the deals might go to waste.

Every program is different, but if you eat out a few times you may accrue savings for future use. Also, if your dining companions don't collect points you may be able to earn theirs, too, depending on the program rules.

TAKE ADVANTAGE OF DAILY DEAL SITES

Check the numerous daily deal sites before eating out. You can usually download your voucher instantly, with no printing necessary — just show it on your smartphone. And if you've left home without that discount dining certificate you bought or you forgot to buy one, don't despair. Just call up your discount certificate on your phone. Or use your phone to buy the certificate on the spot.

Here are several free apps you should not leave home without:

 **Restaurant.com** (*https://livingon thecheap.com/RestaurantCom*) This company sells discounted restaurant certificates. The regular price is $10 for $25 worth of dining, but there are often sales with promo codes that bring the price down to $4 or $5. Once you join the mailing list, Restaurant.com will send you the promo codes.

DAILY DEAL SITES

Groupon, Living Social, Travelzoo and any other daily deal sites active in your city. You can call up certificates you've purchased and buy new ones. On Groupon's app (*https://livingonthecheap.com/Groupon*), for example, you can also see available restaurant deals on a map.

OpenTable

This app (and website; *https://www.opentable.com*) lets you earn points for making reservations at restaurants. Once you earn a certain number of points, you get a certificate for dining dollars good at any participating restaurant. Can you reserve from your phone on the way to dinner? Yes, you can. Once you've earned 2,000 points, you can redeem for a $20 dining check. Even if you are dining alone, make a reservation.

Yelp

Yelp (*https://www.yelp.com*) is great for finding restaurants. You just type in what you're looking for (restaurant, gelato, Greek, pizza) and it comes back with the closest places to you meeting that definition. You can filter by distance, price and other criteria and see either a map or list view. You can also find coupons.

SOCIAL MEDIA

You can also use your phone's Internet browser or your Facebook and Twitter apps to look for restaurant coupons and many restaurants are now creating their own apps and offering discounts and freebies to diners who use them.

One caveat: Not all restaurants are as mobile-savvy as they should be so you may want to ask before you dine or even before you go to ensure they can process a mobile coupon or certificate.'

but has a wider variety of offerings.

- **Buy discounted restaurant gift cards** on the secondary market. People sell unwanted gift cards to various sites, which resell them at a discount to face value. The options available vary and you have to wait for them to arrive in the mail, but there are some good deals to be had.

- **Search for local dining savings programs.** Chicago has Spring Rewards and Table Savvy, and South Florida has LocalDines.com. Some local programs offer double- and triple-point days when you can earn a substantial number of points for future discounts.

Finally, you may also find great coupons, especially for fast food and casual dining spots, in local and community newspapers. The key is to be flexible. As with all savings, you can't be loyal to one restaurant, if you expect to save big bucks.

OTHER WAYS TO DINE ON A DIME

- **Buy the** *Entertainment Book*. While most of the coupons are for fast food, the book does offer some two-for-one fine dining deals. After one meal, you will have paid for the book. Everything else is profit.

- **Buy a gift card during the holidays** (Christmas, Mother's Day, Father's Day) when gift cards are sold at a discount or with a bonus gift card. Save the gift card and use it later. Read all the terms and conditions to make sure you can use the bonus gift card, as most have a specific time frame for use.

- **Purchase discount gift cards** from Costco and Sam's Club. Costco currently sells most $100 gift cards for about $80. Sam's Club doesn't offer as deep a discount,

CHAPTER 14

USING YOUR COUPONS SKILLS TO HELP OTHERS

Why Laura Scours Denver for Toothpaste

Why does Laura run around Denver looking for deals? It's an easy way to give if you are short of money. She is using her coupon skills to get free or nearly free products that charities can share with families in need.

A few weeks ago, I bought 56 tubes of toothpaste, 43 cans of shaving cream and 35 bottles of liquid hand soap. Not that I need 56 tubes of toothpaste, 43 cans of shaving cream and 35 bottles of liquid hand soap, but my favorite local charity does. How much did I spend? Zero. Well, that's not exactly true. I paid, on average, four to six cents per item in sales tax. And these toiletries were fresh off the grocery store shelves, nothing damaged or expired or recalled.

My trick: coupons. The pay-off: a way to use my money-saving skills to benefit others.

Regardless of the season, we all want to help those in need. Using coupons lets you save money when you shop for yourself and also give any extras to nonprofits working to help the underserved, homeless or less fortunate. Many families scramble to keep their pantries and refrigerators filled.

GREAT NEED FOR NON-FOOD ITEMS

Here's something that may surprise: You can't use food stamps to buy toiletries, paper products or cleaning supplies. Because there are so many coupons for these types of products, odds are you can gather coupons that enable you to scoop up needed items for pennies on the dollar.

If you'd like to put your couponing skills to work, first locate a charity. Mine is Families First,

a nonprofit dedicated to ending the cycle of child abuse and neglect through parenting support classes and a residential program for children. A ton of folks come to the Families First center, many who use some form of food assistance. When money is tight, some families have to ration toilet paper or soap. Up to a dozen children may live on site, and as a Families First staffer told me, "We go through 100 to 200 juice boxes and nutritious snack bars a month."

I could just make a donation to the local food bank or Families First. But as a consumer advocate

and executive editor of Living on the Cheap, I know how to stretch every shopping dollar and practice what I preach. So if I can gather $2,000 worth of goods per month for $10 and then donate them, I'm going to do so.

I have one big advantage: I live in Denver. Lucky for me (and other residents of the Mile High City), one of our grocery stores, Safeway, doubles coupons up to $1 every day, 365 days a year. And because I'm in a city with a ton of grocery shopping alternatives — Walmart, Target,, King Soopers (Kroger), Sav-a-Lot, Costco and more — the competition is fierce for my grocery dollar.

DEVISING A STRATEGY

Here's my strategy. Each Sunday, I pull all the coupon inserts from my newspaper. I clip any coupon for items that aren't perishable or really expensive — toiletries, cleaning supplies, canned goods, cereal, snack bars, etc. The manufacturer doesn't matter. On Sunday afternoon, I also try to find any leftover newspapers with extra coupon inserts at local haunts like Starbucks or Panera

Bread (folks tend to read the newspaper over coffee and then leave the papers for others).

In Denver, those of us who subscribe to the Denver Post also get additional coupon inserts on some Wednesdays and Thursdays. And, at the start of each month, I print out coupons from the Living on the Cheap coupon page (*https:// livingonthecheap.com/coupons*).

The last weekend of every month, Procter & Gamble issues a coupon insert. While I get mine in the Sunday newspaper, if I'm lucky, the local free community newspapers will have P&G inserts as well. So the day before those papers get trashed, I scoop them up from kiosks, stands and local businesses and nab extra P&G coupons.

USING YOUR SKILLS TO SAVE MORE

Then comes the strategizing and, sometimes, sheer luck. I sit on those coupons until I find a great deal. For example, every six weeks or so, either Colgate and/or Crest toothpaste is marked down to 99 cents at Safeway. If I'm lucky, I'll have a stash of 50-cent-off toothpaste coupons without restriction.

In other words, the coupon says I can buy any variety of that specific brand of toothpaste. Let's do the math. A 50-cent coupon is doubled to $1. That makes the 99-cent toothpaste free, except for sales tax. That's when I jump in my car and make my way from one store to another. I play by the rules, so only four "like" coupons can be used in a single purchase. If I'm really lucky, I have my friend Lyn with me so we can buy eight tubes per stop.

Toothpaste is fairly straightforward. But what about that hand soap? Aha! Here's where you need to really read the fine print on coupons. P&G often has 50-cent coupons for bars of Ivory soap. Usually there's even a picture of the bars of soap on the coupon. But if you read closely, you'll see that you can use the coupon for any Ivory soap product including the hand soap in a pump bottle. This soap hides amid other more popular brands such as Softsoap or Dial, but to me soap is soap and when it's on sale for 99 cents, I'm on it.

Same for the shaving cream. In that case I reap the rewards when the store has a buy four, get $4 back deal. Usually shaving cream coupons are $1 or $2 off. During the buy four get $4 promotion, that lowers the price of the shaving cream to 99 cents or $1.99, before coupon savings. Other products I can often get for nearly free include deodorant, shampoo, dental floss, boxed macaroni and cheese, ramen-style meals, paper towels, facial tissue, sanitary products, laundry detergent, cake mix and condiments (mustard, ketchup, hot sauce, etc.).

GETTING ITEMS FOR FREE, OR CLOSE TO IT

Not everything I buy is free, but I can often come close. Cereal and snack bars are a good example. Quite often they will go on sale at $1.99 a box and sometimes even less, $1.49 to $1.66. Use a 50-cents-off one box coupon, double it to $1, and I often pay 50 cents for boxes of name-brand cereal

or protein bars.

Another trick: I check out manager's special shelves and clearance racks at grocery stores, drug stores and stores like Bed Bath & Beyond. My BB&B is one of the larger outlets and carries toiletries in addition to all the linens and kitchen gadgets. About twice a year, Bed Bath & Beyond and similar stores clear shelves in what I term a "product dump." Basically, a manufacturer, say Clairol or L'Oreal, notifies the store that certain hair dye colors or make-up shades are being discontinued.

Stores then pull the merchandise and slash

the prices. When I happen to catch one of these sales, I can get boxes of perfectly good hair color (normally $8 to $10) for $1 to $3. Apply those coupons and, again, I'm paying only pennies. Once a puzzled checkout clerk asked me if I was going to try a dozen different "new looks."

In fact, during one recent shopping venture, I stumbled across a clearance of all sorts of normally expensive makeup, something the women who use Families First services really love. As it happens, I had a stash of $3 off coupons for the purchase of two tubes of mascara and $5 off any two facial makeup products.

SAVING 108 PERCENT

I carefully matched items to coupons and took my purchase to the register. As the clerk started ringing up the order and the coupons, we noticed that an additional store special on makeup (not on sale) was being applied, another $4 off every four items. After ringing up about eight coupons, she turned to me and said, "Now I owe you money." So we stopped, even though I still had coupons in my hand. She actually gave me 13 cents and I have a register receipt that says I saved 108%.

Of course, you can apply similar couponing

tricks to your own shopping. But next time you see a buy-one-get-one free deal or coupon for a product you wouldn't use but someone else might, consider making the purchase and then giving the extra to those who really need it. That's a win-win.

COUPON INSIDER TIP

The worst kept secret in town is that Bed Bath & Beyond coupons (printed not digital) NEVER EXPIRE. So don't toss them or give them away. A lesser known fact is that many Bed Bath & Beyond stores now have large toiletry departments with toothpaste, soap, shampoo, cosmetics and everything you'd find in a drugstore, except the pharmacy. And woo-hoo! They accept manufacturer's coupons. Be sure to check their clearance shelves and also look for the yellow price tags, which indicate an item is on deep discount.

CHAPTER 15

READY, SET, CLIP!

See, that wasn't so hard. Now do you understand how you can save hundreds or thousands of dollars by investing, maybe, 30 minutes a week? Beware: Coupon use is addictive. But it pays.

Congratulations! You've made it through our guide. We hope we've inspired you to seek out greater discounts and keep more money in your pocket.

Even if you consider yourself a laid-back coupon clipper, logging five minutes here and there, you can become "dedicated" by spending just 30 minutes per week. Who knows? You may become unstoppable, investing at least an hour a week. Whatever works for you, works for us.

Now that you are a member of the coupon club, seek out others who share your passion and share what you've learned. Host a swap party so everyone can share the coupons they don't want.

Better yet, incorporate coupon trading into a gathering you already attend — such as a play group, soccer game, book club or Scouting event.

Create an informal network of friends and family and email or text each other whenever you spot a fantastic deal. Or turn shopping day into a friends' day out. It's much more fun when you can share in the thrill of saving.

As long as businesses need us to spend, there will always be coupons. Keep those scissors and smartphones handy. Ready, set, save!

We love to hear from committed coupon clippers. Share your tips with us by emailing us at: coupons@livingonthecheap.com

FIND MORE SAVINGS TIPS AT OUR WEBSITES

Living on the Cheap operates a network of more than 30 websites nationwide that provide tips on local deals, discounts and free and cheap things to do. We want you to enjoy your city for less.

Arizona
- Phoenix Living on the Cheap

California
- Orange County on the Cheap
- San Diego on the Cheap.

Colorado
- ~~Mile High on the Cheap~~
- Pikes Peak on the Cheap

District of Columbia
- Washington D.C. on the Cheap

Florida
- Florida On The Cheap
- Florida Keys On The Cheap
- Fort Lauderdale On The Cheap
- Jacksonville On The Cheap
- Miami On The Cheap
- Orlando On The Cheap
- Palm Beach On The Cheap

Georgia
- Atlanta on the Cheap

Illinois
- Chicago on the Cheap

Kansas
- Kansas City on the Cheap
- Wichita on the Cheap

Maryland
- Baltimore on the Cheap

Massachusetts
- Boston Living on the Cheap

Minnesota
- Twin Cities on the Cheap

Missouri
- Kansas City on the Cheap

Nevada
- Vegas Living on the Cheap

New York
- NYC on the Cheap

North Carolina
- Charlotte on the Cheap
- Triangle on the Cheap

Ohio
- Columbus on the Cheap

Oregon
- Portland Living on the Cheap

South Carolina
- Myrtle Beach on the Cheap

Utah
- Salt Lake City on the Cheap

Virginia
- RVA (Richmond) on the Cheap

Washington
- Greater Seattle on the Cheap

IN BETA OR COMING SOON

- Indianapolis on the Cheap
- Los Angeles on the Cheap
- Philadelphia on the Cheap
- Pittsburgh On The Cheap
- Tampa Bay on the Cheap

RESOURCES

- Check this list of current counterfeit coupons
  http://www.couponinformationcenter.com/ psa-list.php

- Ebates app
  https://livingonthecheap.com/ebates

- *Entertainment Book*
  https://livingonthecheap.com/EntertainmentBook

- *Favado*
  https://www.savings.com/favado

- Find a local On the Cheap site
  https://livingonthecheap.com/our-network

- Goldstar
  https://livingonthecheap.com/Goldstar

- Groupon
  https://livingonthecheap.com/Groupon

- Ibotta app
  https://livingonthecheap.com/Ibotta

- Living Social
  https://livingonthecheap.com/LivingSocial

- Living on the Cheap
  https://livingonthecheap.com

- Living On The Cheap coupons page
  http://www.livingonthecheap.com/coupons

- Living on the Cheap's Store Promo Codes page
  https://livingonthecheap.com/PromoCodes

- OpenTable app and website
  https://www.opentable.com

- *Receipt Hog*
  https://receipthog.com

- Restaurant.com
  https://livingonthecheap.com/RestaurantCom

- Share your coupon questions at
  coupons@livingonthecheap.com

- *Shopkick* app
  https://www.shopkick.com

- Subscribe to Living on the Cheap's free national newsletter
  https://livingonthecheap.com/subscribe

- Target Cartwheel app and Website
  https://cartwheel.target.com

- Valpak website
  http://valpak.com

- *Walgreens* app
  https://livingonthecheap.com/walgreensapp

- Yelp
  https://www.yelp.com

ABOUT THE AUTHORS

 **Laura Daily** has risen to the ranks of Jedi Warrior in the fight against the evil empire of high prices. A confirmed coupon clipper, Laura is always on the lookout for ways to save or stretch that hard-earned dollar and prides herself on digging deep to unearth a great deal. Laura lives in Denver, Colorado, and is owner and publisher of *Mile High On The Cheap* and co-owner of Living On The Cheap. She co-authors the popular weekly "Cheap Checklist" column for *The Denver Post* and presents workshops on a variety of money-saving topics. Laura is a consumer advocate and travel strategist reporting for a variety of national publications. For more than a decade she was a Contributing Editor to AARP The Magazine and has also written for *Consumer Reports Money Adviser, Shop Smart* and *All You.* You can reach her at *Laura@milehighonthecheap.com.*

 **Teresa Mears** is a website publisher, writer, content strategist and editor who was raised to be frugal. In her 40 years as a journalist, she has written for papers ranging in size from the weekly *Portland (Tenn.) Leader* to *The Los Angeles Times.* She's editor-in-chief and co-owner of Living on the Cheap. She worked as an editor for *The Miami Herald* for more than 17 years, overseeing coverage of home, real estate, family and other subjects, as well as editing national and international news. She has also been a contributor to *The New York Times, The Boston Globe* and other publications. When she's not writing about Florida deals, she writes for *U.S. News & World Report.* Teresa operates the On the Cheap websites in Florida, including *Miami On The Cheap,* and *Fort Lauderdale On The Cheap*. You can reach her at *Teresa@livingonthecheap.com.*

Bryan K. Chavez joined Mile High On The Cheap in 2011 as its Senior Editor and co-authors the weekly "Cheap Checklist" column for *The Denver Post.* Bryan also writes "The Coupon Insider" for Living On The Cheap. He never pays full price for anything because he always looks for a coupon, sale or promo before opening his wallet. His deal-seeking skills are so sharp that he regularly saves upwards of 75% on his groceries. (He's the rarely seen male shopping with a coupon binder!) When he's not clipping coupons or searching for a discount, he enjoys going to the movies, listening to Prince music and searching the Internet for cat videos. His educational background is in journalism and public relations.

CPSIA information can be obtained
at www.ICGtesting.com
Printed in the USA
LVIC06n1045131017
552247LV00010B/9